level
3

Vikings

Philip Steele

First published 2013 by Kingfisher
an imprint of Macmillan Children's Books
a division of Macmillan Publishers Limited
20 New Wharf Road, London N1 9RR
Basingstoke and Oxford
Associated companies throughout the world
www.panmacmillan.com

Series editor: Heather Morris
Literacy consultant: Hilary Horton

ISBN: 978-0-7534-3092-7
Copyright © Macmillan Publishers Ltd 2013

9 8 7 6 5 4 3 2 1

1TR/1012/WKT/UG/105MA

A CIP catalogue record for this book is available from
the British Library.

Printed in China

Picture credits
The Publisher would like to thank the following for permission to reproduce their
material. Every care has been taken to trace copyright holders. However, if there
have been unintentional omissions or failure to trace copyright holders, we apologize
and will, if informed, endeavour to make corrections in any future edition.
Top = t; Bottom = b; Centre = c; Left = l; Right = r
Cover Kingfisher; Pages 7 Peter Kuiper/Wikipedia;
9t Corbis/Werner Forman Archive; 9b Shutterstock/Kristina Postnikova; 12 Shutterstock/Mircea
Bezergheanu; 15t Art Archive/ Oldsaksammlung, Oslo/Dagli Orti; 15b Corbis/Werner Forman Archive;
17 Corbis/Werner Forman Archive; 19 Corbis/Werner Forman Archive; 20 Alamy/Troy GB Images;
23 Corbis/Ted Spiegel; 26 Corbis/Ted Spiegel; 28 Art Archive/ Musee de la Tapisserie/Gianni Dagli Orti;
all other illustrations from the Kingfisher archive

Contents

Viking tales   4

Who were the Vikings?   6

Gods and giants   8

In the longhouse   10

Farming and food   12

Making beautiful things   14

Towns and trade   16

Going to sea   18

Warriors and weapons   20

Raiders and settlers   22

Sailing west   24

Burials and burnings   26

The end of an age   28

Glossary   30

Index   32

Viking tales

Norway, Sweden and Denmark are lands in the north of Europe. They have rocky coasts. There are mountains, lakes and big forests. The winters are cold and snowy, but the summers are warm.

The people who lived in these lands between about 750 and 1100CE are known as Vikings. They were farmers, fishermen, traders and fighters.

Viking men fought for their local **chief**, the **jarl**. Sometimes the jarl called his people to the great hall. They feasted, drinking ale or wine. Often a poet called a **skald** told exciting tales about battles, ships, treasure and monsters.

Finding out

Many old Viking stories were eventually written down. If we read these **sagas** today, we can find out how the Vikings lived long ago.

Who were the Vikings?

The name Viking means 'sea-raider'. More than 1,200 years ago Viking warriors began to sail far from their homes. They raided towns and villages. They seized gold from churches, burned buildings and stole cattle. They killed people or carried them off as **slaves**.

The Vikings travelled far and wide, exploring and settling new lands. They were not just fighters, they also cleared forests, farmed the land and fished.

There were many successful Viking traders, as well as expert craft workers. Viking settlers built towns and passed laws.

Viking writing
The Vikings spoke a language we call Old Norse. It was sometimes written down in letters called **runes**. You can see runes on this stone.

Gods and giants

Vikings believed in many gods. Odin was the father of the gods. People believed that he rode an eight-legged horse. On stormy nights they thought they could see him galloping across the sky. Odin had two pet **ravens**. They flew around the world each day and told him what they saw.

God of thunder

This is a carving of Thor, who was the god of thunder and lightning. He had a big hammer, which he used to fight giants and monsters.

The Vikings believed in other worlds, too, where there were giants, monsters, snakes and spirits. At the centre of the universe was a gigantic ash tree, called Yggdrasil (say IG-druh-sil).

The way to the gods

Vikings believed that the world of humans was joined to the world of the gods by a great rainbow bridge.

In the longhouse

Many Vikings lived in farming **settlements**, with stables, barns and cowsheds. The biggest building was the longhouse. This long wooden hut had a **thatched** roof.

Inside, it was dark and smoky. A fire burned in the hearth and the floor was covered with rushes. Weapons hung on the walls. Platforms along the walls were used as beds or seats. Families, farm workers and slaves all slept here. Women prepared food, span wool and wove cloth on a loom. The men repaired fishing lines, tools or weapons.

Games and dice
On winter nights Vikings sat by the fire and played dice or board games such as chess.

11

Farming and food

Viking farmers grew wheat, barley, rye, peas and cabbages. They raised geese, sheep, goats, pigs, horses and cattle. The animals gave them eggs, milk, meat, wool and leather.

The Vikings also caught wild birds, reindeer and wild **boar**. The seas were full of cod and herring, which they caught in nets.

Farmers raised goats for meat and milk.

People often salted or dried meat and fish to eat in winter. They cooked over a fire, on hot stones, or stewed food in **cauldrons**.

13

Making beautiful things

Viking women wove thread into cloth to make clothes and blankets. They wore a simple, long dress with a long tunic over it. The shoulder straps were fastened with beautiful **brooches** and chains.

Men wore long **breeches** and woollen tunics.

The Vikings were clever **smiths** and metal workers. They made jewellery from gold, silver, yellow **amber** and shiny black **jet**. Viking craftsmen carved horn, walrus tusks, wood and stone.

This wood carving shows a smith making a fine sword.

Pictures and patterns

Viking designs had swirling patterns and knots, with birds, snakes and monsters.

Towns and trade

Most towns
were built by rivers or
harbours so boats could
carry goods and people. There were
few proper roads in Viking times.

Houses and workshops were made of wood.
People dug ditches or built fences around
the town as defences if they were attacked
by enemies. Towns had markets, where

people bought
food, tools, pots and
pans or jewellery.

Traders went on
long journeys –
some went to Russia
for furs and some
went south, to buy
silks and spices.

Goods and money
At first people just
exchanged goods
at market. About a
thousand years ago,
the Vikings began
to make their
own coins.

Going to sea

The Vikings built many types of boat, from little rowing boats to sturdy ships which carried heavy **cargo**. Their finest ships were 23 metres long. These **longships** were used for crossing the oceans or going to war.

Viking longships were sleek and fast, and shallow enough to row up a river. Each ship had a crew of 30 or more men, who rowed the ship. Every man had one oar. The ship had a square sail made of wool or linen.

All the sailors were also fighters, and they were heavily armed. They hung shields along the sides of the ship to protect the rowers from enemy arrows.

Dragon ships
Longships had a high wooden **prow**. It was often carved into a snarling dragon shape to scare the enemy.

Warriors and weapons

Most Vikings were farmers and fishermen who joined their jarl for raids. Later, some hired themselves out as fighting men, or joined other Vikings to form large armies.

Warriors wore everyday clothes into battle, and a helmet made of leather or iron. Jarls often wore mail shirts made from iron rings.

Vikings fought with iron swords, spears, axes, bows and arrows. Their big, round shields were made of wood, with an iron knob in the middle.

Berserk!
Some warriors worked themselves into a fury before a battle. They were called 'berserkir', and they wore shirts of bear skin. Today we still use the word berserk to mean crazy.

Raiders and settlers

Viking raiders left home in search of **plunder**. They wanted to be rich and powerful. Vikings attacked villages, towns and even big cities. They attacked Britain, Ireland, Germany, France and Spain.

The Vikings set up winter camps in foreign lands. Then they built new settlements overseas and took control of whole regions.

York in England became a Viking city called Jorvik. In France, the Vikings won a large area of land called Normandy.

Archaeologists find Viking remains under the streets of Dublin, in Ireland.

Nicknames
Viking warriors had scary nicknames, such as Erik Bloodaxe and Thorfinn Skull-Splitter.

Sailing west

The Vikings sailed west across the oceans. Between 874 and 930CE they settled in Iceland. There were few trees, so they built longhouses from stone and turf. Wherever they settled, they set up assemblies to make laws and solve arguments.

Sometimes storms blew Viking longships even further west and the sailors sighted unknown lands.

Viking assemblies were held in the open air.

Viking settlers hunted walrus and seals off the icy coasts of Greenland.

In 982CE Erik the Red led settlers to an icy land. He called it Greenland, hoping that this name would attract more people.

Erik's son was Leif the Lucky. In about 1002CE he sailed down the coast of Canada, reaching a place he called Vinland. The

Vikings tried to settle in North America, but they were fiercely attacked by the **native Americans**.

Burials and burnings

Vikings returned from their travels with lots of treasure. In times of war or trouble, they buried the treasure to keep it safe. People discover these secret hoards today.

A Viking hoard (hidden store) found in Sweden

In the hall of Odin
Vikings believed that warriors who died in battle met the god Odin. They feasted forever in his great hall, Valholl.

Archaeologists also find treasure
in places where Vikings were buried.
Some dead Viking chieftains were
put in their ship, which was set on fire.
Others were placed inside a wooden
ship and buried beneath a mound
of earth.

The end of an age

After about 960CE, many Vikings became Christians. The new faith spread slowly. For some years people wore the hammer symbol of the god Thor alongside the cross of Christianity. By the 1080s, all the Viking lands were Christian.

The lands of the local jarls became part of large Christian kingdoms. Vikings served

When the Normans invaded Britain in 1066, their boats looked just like Viking longships.

in big armies. Descendants of the Vikings who settled in France, called Normans, conquered large parts of Europe, from England to Italy. The old Viking lands make up the modern countries of Denmark, Sweden, Norway and Iceland.

VIKING DATES

789	Vikings start to raid the British Isles.
841	Vikings are based in Dublin, Ireland.
867	Vikings capture York (Jorvik), England.
874	Vikings settle Iceland.
911	Vikings win Normandy, in France.
960	Christianity starts in Viking lands.
982	Erik the Red reaches Greenland.
1002	Leif the Lucky explores Vinland (Newfoundland, Canada).
c.1100	The Viking age comes to an end.

Glossary

amber A yellow-brown fossil resin, often used to make jewellery or other precious items.

archaeologist Someone who digs up and studies ancient ruins and remains.

boar A wild pig.

breeches Trousers.

brooch An ornamental pin or fastener.

cargo Goods loaded on a ship.

cauldron A big metal cooking pot.

chief The powerful leader of a region.

harbour A place where ships shelter and are prepared for their journeys.

jarl A Viking chieftain or nobleman.

jet A shiny black stone.

longship A long, narrow ship with oars and a single sail.

native Americans The peoples who first lived in North America.

plunder To steal goods during war.

prow The front of a ship

ravens Big black birds in the crow family.

runes The letters of the Viking alphabet.

saga An exciting story or history.

settlements Places where people live and have built houses and other buildings.

skald A Viking poet and storyteller.

slave A person who is owned by someone else and made to work for no money.

smiths Craftspeople who work with iron or other metals.

thatched Covered with straw or reed.

Index

animals 8, 12, 25
assemblies 24

clothing 14, 20, 21

Erik the Red 25

farmers 12, 20
food 11, 12, 13, 17

gods 8–9, 26, 28

jarls 5, 20, 21
jewellery 15, 17

Leif the Lucky 25
longhouses 10, 16, 24

longships 18, 19, 27, 28

markets 16, 17
money 17

raids 6, 22
runes 7

sagas 5
settlers 7, 22, 24, 25

slaves 6, 11

traders 17
treasure 26, 27

warriors 20, 21, 23